Where Is
Walt Disney
World®?

by Joan Holub

illustrated by Gregory Copeland

Penguin Workshop
An Imprint of Penguin Random House

For Russell Street School, St. Patrick's School,
Pine Road Elementary, Polytechnic School, and
Monroe Elementary—JH

For my brother Michael—GC

PENGUIN WORKSHOP
Penguin Young Readers Group
An Imprint of Penguin Random House LLC

Library of Congress Cataloging-in-Publication Data is available.

ISBN 9780515158434 (paperback)   10 9 8 7 6 5 4 3 2 1
ISBN 9780515158458 (library binding)   10 9 8 7 6 5 4 3 2 1

Contents

Where Is Walt Disney World? 1

Walt Disney 6

Building Disney World 20

Magic Kingdom 30

Behind the Scenes 47

Epcot 58

Animal Kingdom 66

Hollywood Studios 76

Changes and Updates 82

Water Parks, Parades, Fireworks, and More 90

After-the-Park Fun 99

Timelines 106

Bibliography 108

Where Is Walt Disney World?

It was 1964, and someone was buying land in Central Florida—a lot of land, for cheap. Much of it was cow pastures or swamps. Land like this was nothing special and only cost about $180 an acre. Who would want so much of it?

Maybe a big business was coming to Florida and bringing jobs. Rumors flew. Would it be Ford? General Electric? NASA?

On October 24, 1965, a local newspaper called the *Orlando Sentinel* solved the mystery. It blasted this headline: "We Say: 'Mystery' Industry Is Disney." This was great news. Everyone knew about the famous Disneyland theme park in Anaheim, California, on the West Coast of the United States. Walt Disney must be planning to build an East Coast Disneyland, too!

This turned out to be true, sort of. In fact, Walt Disney and his brother Roy had decided to build a bigger version of Disneyland in Florida. There would be lots of changes. The official name would end up as Walt Disney World® Resort, commonly called Disney World for short.

Back in November of 1963, Walt had chosen Central Florida for the new theme park. The area had sunny weather, with average temperatures in the 60s in winter and 80s in summer. It was near the crossing of Interstate 4 and Florida's Turnpike, and there was a regional airport about a half hour away. Getting to Disney World would be an easy trip by car or airplane.

However, if anyone had guessed what Walt was up to, land prices would have soared sky-high. Many people knew what Walt looked like from the TV show he hosted on ABC. So he and Roy, who were business partners, had to be clever. They didn't personally contact landowners and ask to buy their property. They had other people do that. Besides the Disney brothers, only five others were let in on the plan, which they called "Project X" or the "Florida Project."

Using made-up company names like Tomahawk Properties, they quietly began buying land. If Walt or Roy went to Florida during this time, they used fake names like Walt and Roy Davis. These initials (W. D. and R. D.) matched the ones that were monogrammed on their suitcases.

Such tricks worked—for a while. That was lucky, because after the news got out that Disney was the buyer, land prices in the area shot up to $1,000 an acre. In all, the company had bought about 27,440 acres (forty-three square miles) in Florida by then. That's almost twice the size of Manhattan in New York City!

There was no doubt about it. Walt Disney was thinking big!

Where to Find Disney World

Disney World is located about twenty miles southwest of Orlando. That's the closest big city, so you'll often hear people say it's *in* Orlando. Actually, Disney World's mailing address and some of its properties are in nearby Lake Buena Vista, Florida. Yet all four of its theme parks are in the city of Bay Lake, next door.

CHAPTER 1
Walt Disney

Walter Elias Disney was born more than one hundred years ago on December 5, 1901, in Chicago, Illinois. He grew up on a farm near Marceline, Missouri, with three older brothers and a younger sister.

Walt was a boy with imagination and talent. He would gaze up at the clouds and imagine them slowly changing from one animal shape into another. Once, he got in trouble for painting pictures all over the outside of the family's white house with black tar.

In Marceline, most people figured he would become an artist because he drew all the time.

He and his brother Roy, who was eight years older than Walt, were good friends. Their family

didn't have much money, and their father was strict. Roy was almost like a second dad to Walt sometimes, making sure he got a toy or some candy on his birthday.

Growing up on a farm, the brothers learned the importance of hard work, and they never forgot it. Walt fell in love with trains when he got a summer job selling snacks and newspapers to passengers.

Much later on, Walt even built a small train in his backyard for his family. All his life, he remained a kid at heart.

As a boy, Walt was always drawing—even in the margins of his schoolbooks to turn them into flip-books. In high school, he took art classes at night. During World War I, Walt drove a Red Cross ambulance he decorated with cartoons.

He dreamed of making films and doing new things with animation. In 1923, he moved to Hollywood, where he and Roy began the Disney Brothers Cartoon Studio. Today, the official Disney Fan Club is called D23. *D* for Disney and *23* for 1923, because that year was an important turning point.

Roy O. Disney (1893–1971)

Roy and Walt were very different. Roy was quiet, smart about money, and camera-shy. Walt was creative and outgoing. As boys, Walt and Roy shared a bed in the attic of their family's house. In 1923, Roy and Walt lived in a one-room apartment where Roy did all the cooking.

Walt and Roy would disagree and argue at times. But even if he disagreed with one of Walt's ideas, Roy would usually support him. Roy believed in Walt. He also thought Walt was too trusting sometimes, and tried to protect him from any clever crooks. By making good business deals for their company, Roy gave Walt the time and freedom to make his dreams come true.

In a speech Walt once said, "In my career, it helps to have some kind of genius. I've got it but it happens to be in the person of my brother Roy, who runs the company . . ."

Roy and his wife had one son, also named Roy, who worked at Disney when he grew up. Roy Disney died on December 20, 1971, about three months after Disney World opened.

Walt Disney won many honors, including thirty-two Academy Awards, the most ever in history. One of his honorary awards was in 1932 for the creation of Mickey Mouse! Disney's *Snow*

White and the Seven Dwarfs was the very first full-length animated musical film. It was a huge success. The golden award Walt received for the film included seven little statuettes to represent the dwarfs.

Over the next five years, Disney created more classic full-length animated films, including *Pinocchio*, *Fantasia*, *Dumbo,* and *Bambi.* Of course, he would go on to do much more.

Walt married Lillian Bounds, an animator working for his company, in 1925. He liked to take their two daughters, Diane and Sharon, to ride a merry-go-round in Griffith Park near the famous Hollywood

Lillian Bounds

sign. As he waited for them on a nearby bench, he wished there was a place that had entertaining activities for both the young and the young-at-heart. This wish would eventually spark the idea of creating a theme park.

Amusement parks had been around for a long time. Tivoli Gardens in Copenhagen, Denmark, opened in 1843, with fabulous gardens and two amazing mechanical attractions—a roller coaster and a carousel.

Luna Park (1903) and Dreamland (1904) opened at Coney Island, New York, when Walt was a little boy. Their attractions introduced visitors to foreign or imaginary lands. You could ride an elephant from India or blast off on a pretend trip to the moon, or go on a gondola ride called Canals of Venice.

But no one had ever built a theme park that was all about cartoon and fairy-tale characters, until Walt.

Luna Park

Making *Snow White and the Seven Dwarfs*

During the making of the movie *Snow White* in 1937, Walt would play-act roles for Disney animators to explain how he wanted the characters to behave. To draw Snow White dancing in a scene, animators watched film of a woman dancing. To draw the dwarfs' goofy expressions, the artists would watch themselves make goofy expressions in a mirror.

Animals were kept at the studio during production so artists could draw them, too.

Animators drew black-and-white outlines of the characters on transparent sheets called cels. Background cels were created separately from the character cels. Women in the ink-and-paint department painted colors on the back side of the cels, filling the spaces inside the black outlines like in a coloring book. They also got the brilliant idea to paint actual makeup on Snow White's face. This gave her a rosy, natural look in the film. The finished cels were photographed in sequence. When they were shown rapidly, the characters on them appear to move, much like in a flip-book.

CHAPTER 2
Building Disney World

About three weeks after everyone found out Disney was buying all that Florida property, there was a press conference. Walt said the new park would be the "biggest thing we've ever tackled."

At Disney World, he planned to include some of Disneyland's most popular attractions. One was called "it's a small world." On the ride, visitors sailed past three hundred or so cute singing, dancing dolls representing different countries. The ride's upbeat song was about worldwide friendship.

Walt had plenty of epic new ideas for Disney World, too. But there were things he didn't want—like the kind of hotels, shops, and restaurants that had sprung up around Disneyland. They were crowded all around the park, leaving no room for it to expand. In Florida, he would finally have all the land he needed.

Unfortunately, he would never see his new ideas built. In 1966, Walt Disney died of lung cancer. Many Americans, and

Walt Disney dies at age 65

everyone at Disney, were stunned and terribly sad. Walt was one of a kind. He was charming and popular. He was the idea man. How could Disney continue without him? Roy had been in charge of the financial side of the business, but he was retiring.

Now what?

Since the Disney World project had been so important to Walt, Roy decided that retirement would have to wait. He was determined to make the new park happen. Without Roy, Disney World would not have been built.

The job would be huge and overwhelming, almost like organizing many battles for a war. Two military men were put in charge, Admiral Joe Fowler and General Joe Potter.

Joe Fowler

Joe Fowler was an architect-engineer who had served in the navy designing and building ships. He knew how to manage large projects and groups of workers. He had already helped Walt build Disneyland and find the land for Disney World.

Walt had always insisted on the best for his projects. He didn't like to be told that something would cost too much or that it couldn't be done. Joe Fowler was a can-do type of guy. Once, when Walt told him he wanted a waterfall in Adventureland to part so that cast members could come out through it, Joe replied, "Can do." Even though he likely had no idea how to make Walt's idea work, he figured out a way!

Joe Potter had been in the army, and was an expert engineer. Potter was put in charge of bringing electrical power and water to Disney World.

Joe Potter

After the design phase, construction began. Swampland had to be drained and dirt moved. Trees had to be moved or cut down.

The area was huge and it was hard to imagine where everything would go. Colored gas balloons on long strings were tied to the ground here and there to show the height and placement of future landmarks like Cinderella Castle. Building Disney World would take more than four years.

Disney World finally opened on October 1, 1971. Walt's dream had come true. Or had it? Just ten thousand guests came! *Uh-oh.* That was only about twice the number of cast members working at the park. Some people predicted Walt's second park was going to fail. However, it turned out that Disney World had purposely opened off-season, when fewer people went on vacation. This would allow more time to work out any kinks before bigger crowds came. And come they did. In 2016, a total of more than fifty-three million people visited Walt Disney World's four parks!

In 1971, a ticket to Disney World for ages three through eleven cost a dollar, plus three dollars and fifty cents for tickets to seven rides. Magic Kingdom was its only theme park at first. Epcot was added in 1982, Hollywood Studios (originally named Disney-MGM Studios) in 1989, and Animal Kingdom in 1998.

They're called theme parks because most of what's in each park is built around a main theme or idea. Today, a one-day Magic Kingdom ticket can cost ninety-nine dollars or more.

Originally, Walt's plan had been to name his Florida location simply Disney World. However, Roy wanted to honor his brother and help people remember him. Today, the official name Roy chose decorates the brightly colored entrance signs on the road into the resort that read, "Walt Disney World: Where Dreams Come True."

Disneyland

Sixteen years before Disney World, Walt built his first theme park: Disneyland. It was to be a new kind of amusement park where kids and grown-ups could all have family fun. They could meet Mickey Mouse and other Disney cartoon and fairy-tale characters and ride a train like the ones from Marceline. Would the idea work? Before building Disneyland, Walt studied the competition. Their amusement parks were mostly messy and dirty. Their workers didn't seem happy or friendly. He knew he could do better.

Disneyland took a year to build and opened on July 17, 1955, in Anaheim, California, near Los Angeles. There were big problems on its first day. Some rides were broken or not ready. Someone had printed and sold thousands of fake admission tickets, so the crowds were unexpectedly huge.

It was hot—one hundred degrees! There wasn't enough water. The new asphalt walkways turned gooey, and people's shoes got stuck. It wasn't long until everything was running smoothly, though. Now Disneyland is called "The Happiest Place on Earth." There are also other Disneylands in Europe and Asia.

CHAPTER 3
Magic Kingdom

Of all the Disney World parks, Magic Kingdom gets the most visitors. In fact, it gets more visitors annually than any other theme park in the world! You enter it on Main Street, U.S.A., which looks like a street in a small American town from the year 1900.

Some of the buildings were modeled after the Missouri town where Walt and Roy grew up. Windows in the stores along the street are built low, so children can look inside. Here, you can board railroad trains for a ride around the Magic Kingdom. The red train is named for Walt. The green one is Lilly Belle, named for his wife.

At the far end of Main Street stands Cinderella Castle, soaring high with twenty-seven royal-blue and gold towers and four turrets. It was inspired by European castles, and has a drawbridge and a water-filled moat. Though they look like stone, the "marble bricks" are actually fiberglass panels attached to a steel frame then coated with plaster and concrete. The towers were built on the ground, then lifted by cranes into place.

For flight safety, federal law says that any building more than two hundred feet tall must display a flashing red light on top. Since that would have spoiled the fairy-tale effect, Cinderella Castle is only 189 feet tall. It looks much taller, though, due to the use of forced perspective. The "bricks" and windows higher up are smaller than those at the bottom. This fools your eyes into seeing the castle as much taller than it really is!

From the Cinderella Castle area, paths branch out to Magic Kingdom's six lands. Clockwise they are Fantasyland, Tomorrowland, Main Street, Adventureland, Frontierland, and Liberty Square.

Fantasyland is all about magic and fairy tales, just like many of Walt's films. It has four castles: Cinderella Castle, Prince Eric's Castle, Beast's Castle, and Rapunzel's tower.

Rapunzel's tower

Mickey Mouse

Of all Walt Disney's characters, Mickey Mouse is the best loved and most well-known. Walt said that Mickey Mouse popped out of his mind during a train ride in 1928. He was going to name him Mortimer, until his wife, Lillian, suggested

the name Mickey. That same year, Mickey debuted in a short cartoon called *Plane Crazy*. It was black and white, without sound. In those days, theater owners showed short cartoons before a full-length movie. However, no one was interested in Mickey. Walt didn't give up.

Soon he featured Mickey in another short called *Steamboat Willie*. It was a hit! Mickey whistled merrily, and his friend Minnie said, "Yoo-hoo!" This was the first cartoon with sound matched to the characters, making them almost appear to be talking. Walt himself would perform the high-pitched voice of Mickey in more than one hundred cartoon shorts.

Over time, Mickey's appearance changed a little. His tail disappeared and he got white gloves. Today, Mickey Mouse is one of the most recognizable characters in the world. In China, he's *Mi Lao Shu*; in Italy he's *Topolino*; and in Mexico, he's *Ratón Mickey*. Walt Disney once said this about his huge success: "It was all started by a mouse."

The Prince Charming Regal Carrousel in this land is a real antique from 1917. At sixty feet across, it's one of the biggest of its kind in the world. Its ninety wooden horses on golden poles are decorated with colorful bridles, flowers, and shields.

When the Disney Company bought the carousel in 1967, its horses were covered in many old layers of paint. After sanding that off, they were painted white because most heroes rode white horses in movies and fairy tales.

Many of the "cars" in Disney World rides are cleverly designed. In Magic Kingdom, you ride in clamshells at Under the Sea—Journey of the Little Mermaid. Dumbo the Flying Elephant has cute elephant-shaped cars that "fly." The Seven Dwarfs Mine Train roller coaster's cars sway side to side like cars in a real mine shaft.

Tomorrowland's theme is outer space and aliens. It has the first computer-controlled thrill ride—Space Mountain. This roller coaster is popular and superfast. In the 1960s there was a space race to see which country—the United States or the USSR—would land on the moon first. On July 20, 1969, about two years before Disney World opened, American astronauts became the first to walk on the moon.

People remained fascinated by
the idea of outer space and what
might be discovered there.
So that is what inspired
Tomorrowland.

Space Mountain

Walt was optimistic and excited about new technology, and thought it would help the world in the future. At the Carousel of Progress, the audience sits in seats that automatically rotate around a stage to discover how technology has progressed through time. Onstage, an Audio-Animatronic American family discusses four eras, including: 1900—gas lamps, hand-cranked washing machines; 1920s—electricity for lamps, radios; 1940s—TVs, dishwashers. At first, the present-day part of the show presented trends of the 1960s and '70s, such as caring for the environment and moms working outside the home. Today, it highlights high-tech things like virtual-reality games and HD TVs.

Hand-cranked washing machine

Adventureland has a tropical jungle theme, inspired by Africa, Asia, the Carribean, and the South Seas. Jungle Cruise is a lazy outdoor boat ride through this land.

Walt had hoped to have real jungle animals here, but decided they might not behave or might hide when they heard people coming.

Frontierland is set in the Wild West days of the United States. In the 1950s and '60s, there was a craze of cowboy- and Western-themed TV shows. Walt Disney tapped into it by creating a TV show based on a real frontiersman named Davy Crockett. Many kids wanted coonskin caps like the one Davy wore.

The different lands show that Walt wasn't just interested in fairy tales and fantasy. He also wanted to present moments in history, important present-day ideas, and an introduction to other parts of the world.

CHAPTER 4
Behind the Scenes

It takes over seventy thousand cast members to make the magic happen at Disney World. Before beginning their job, most take classes at Disney University, located behind the Magic Kingdom. They learn about Walt Disney, Disney World Resort, Disney characters, and how to behave with guests. After that, there's more training about how to do a particular job, and how to look and act the part of the character they'll portray. (Often one cast member switches roles on different days.)

Unofficial and Official Disney Lingo

Adventure—a ride

Attraction—a ride or a show

Backstage—any part of Disney World that guests cannot see

Cast member—a Disney World employee; CM for short

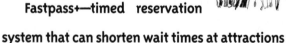

Character—costumed employee acting as a Disney character

Face character—characters like Cinderella and Snow White whose costumes don't cover their heads

Fastpass+—timed reservation system that can shorten wait times at attractions

Flume—water-chute ride

Good show—when a cast member behaves in a friendly, kind manner toward guests or performs a job or character well when in view of guests

Guest—visitor

Imagineers—Disney employees who come up with creative and technical ideas

Lost parent—since kids might get scared if referred to as "lost," the parents are referred to as "lost" instead

MagicBand—colorful wristband used as an admission ticket and more

Onstage—any part of Disney World that guests can see

Queue—line of people waiting to enter an attraction (say: KEW)

Rope drop—nickname for the time Disney World officially opens each morning, because guests sometimes stand behind an actual rope until Disney employees move it aside for them to pass

Utilidors—nickname for employees-only underground tunnels, also called utilities corridors

Disney employees are called cast members for a reason. Walt wanted them to think of themselves as actors in a big show called Disney World. Anytime they are among park guests, even if they are not on a real stage, they are considered to be acting out a role. Even small things are important. Giving directions to a guest by pointing the way with a finger might be considered "bad show." Gesturing the way with a friendly open hand is called "good show." Cast members are expected to be cheerful and polite, which is, of course, "good show"!

Have you ever wondered how Disney characters seem to magically appear in their correct lands? Or why you don't ever see them where they don't belong? Well, one time at Disneyland, Walt caught sight of a cowboy cast member walking through Tomorrowland on the way over to Frontierland. It felt so out of place to Walt. It spoiled the magical feeling he wanted for guests.

So at Disney World, there are underground tunnels for cast members. They walk through them to get to their lands without guests seeing them. The tunnels, called utilidors, form one big circle under the Magic Kingdom with a connecting tunnel going under Main Street through the middle.

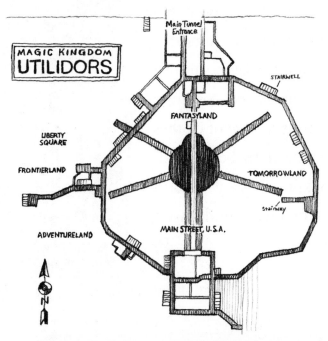

MAGIC KINGDOM
UTILIDORS

Main Tunnel Entrance

STAIRWELL

FANTASYLAND

LIBERTY SQUARE

FRONTIERLAND

TOMORROWLAND

Stairway

ADVENTURELAND

MAIN STREET, U.S.A.

N

If you were a cast member, you'd likely park in a lot about a mile away and take a bus to the tunnel entrance. Your first stop inside the tunnel might be the Mouseketeria for a snack. Across the hall is the wardrobe department. You tell them your size and where you'll be working that day. After you're given a costume, you change and store your belongings in locker rooms.

Mickey Mouse has about 136 outfits, including a tuxedo and a scuba-suit. Minnie Mouse has more than one hundred, including a safari suit. All the characters' costumes amount to a *lot* of clothes that need to be washed. Luckily, Disney World has its own laundries on site.

It is a ten-minute walk from one end of the park to the other going through the tunnels. The tunnels are color-coded and have signs saying which section of the park is directly above.

To get into the land you want, you take an elevator or stairs up one floor. You exit into the Magic Kingdom through one of twenty-nine unmarked doors.

Imagine how hard it might be to remain cheerful on a hot summer day if you're wearing a costume that covers you head to toe! There are rules to make sure cast members get enough breaks. To relax, they might come back downstairs to one of the break rooms.

Because of the tunnels, you won't see garbage trucks in the park emptying trash bins. Instead, trash gets sucked from the park down through twenty-inch pipes at speeds of up to sixty miles an hour. In the tunnels, you can sometimes hear trash flying by on its way to a central collection area.

There are also offices, storage areas, kitchens, a hair salon, makeup rooms, plus design and rehearsal spaces. The park's computer system, Digital Animation Control System (DACS), is here, too. It operates and monitors sound systems, Audio-Animatronic characters, and attractions. It helps make sure stage curtains open on time and parades are on schedule.

Delivery trucks arrive at the tunnels bringing both merchandise and food that eventually get distributed to the parks. Utility workers drive around on golf carts. The tunnels are a busy place!

Audio-Animatronics

Walt was always asking his team of Imagineers to accomplish tasks that seemed impossible. When he found a mechanical singing bird in a store, he showed it to them. They took it apart to see how it worked. Before you knew it, he had them busy building a nine-inch-tall dancing man. This was an early prototype of Audio-Animatronics, which are basically robots. Enchanted Tiki Room opened at Disneyland in 1963, and was the first attraction with Audio-Animatronics. Its tropical birds could do simple actions like open and close their beaks. For the 1964 World's Fair in New York City, Walt created a full-size Audio-Animatronic human figure— Abraham Lincoln. Abe could talk and do fifty-seven movements. In the 1960s, this was new, amazing stuff.

CHAPTER 5
Epcot

Walt Disney hoped Epcot would be the most important part of Disney World. Epcot is a made-up word that stands for **E**xperimental **P**rototype **C**ommunity **of** **T**omorrow. It was meant to be a new futuristic kind of city where people would actually live and work. From overhead, his Epcot plan looked like a wagon wheel.

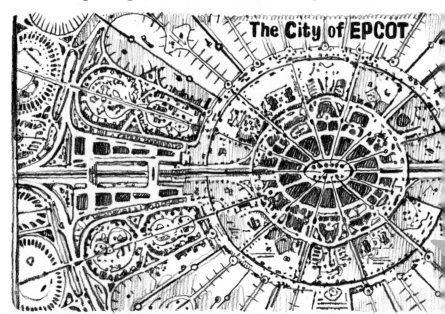

The City of EPCOT

Businesses would be located at its center and surrounded by apartments, parks, and residential neighborhoods. A giant transparent dome would cover the whole city to keep out rain and regulate the temperature inside. Three underground levels would allow travel by trucks, cars, or monorails.

Walt had planned to invite businesses to Epcot that would investigate new technologies and solutions for better ways of living. If these new ideas worked well inside Epcot, they might be used to improve other cities outside the dome, too. Maybe Epcot could change the world!

After Walt died, the Disney company decided it would be too hard to run a real city. Today, Epcot is different from Walt's plan. However, the focus of its two main sections remains technology and the future, things dear to Walt's heart.

As you might guess from its name, Future World has futuristic attractions. Spaceship Earth is a 183-foot-tall, sixteen-million-pound ball balanced on six legs at the entrance to Epcot.

It's called a geosphere, which is a word that means "solid earth." Its outer shell is made of 11,324 lightweight aluminum triangles that shimmer in the light. The ride inside the sphere tells

Ray Bradbury

a brief history of technology and considers what future technologies might be invented. The famous sci-fi writer Ray Bradbury helped create this story.

The Mission: SPACE ride gives you an idea of what it might be like to be an astronaut heading for Mars. You learn food facts and see

Mickey-shaped pumpkins on a Living with the Land boat ride. Many of the fruits and vegetables grown in the greenhouses here are served in Epcot restaurants.

The Seas with Nemo & Friends includes a shell-mobile ride past an aquarium where animated sea creatures appear to swim with real dolphins, rays, and even clownfish like Nemo.

But there is also important wildlife conservation going on at times. In 2010, sixty sea turtles injured by an oil spill in the Gulf of Mexico came to the aquarium to get much-needed help. Why is Future World the home of this kind of work? Maybe because animals are an important part of our Earth's future.

World Showcase brings different cultures from around the world to kids. If you haven't traveled much yet, this is a great way to get a look at what many countries and the people in them are like. Countries include Canada, China, France, Germany, Italy, Japan, Mexico, Morocco, Norway, the United States, and the United Kingdom.

Buildings called pavilions each feature food, exhibits, entertainment, and souvenirs related to one country. There's a small version of the Eiffel Tower in the France pavilion and mosaics in the Morocco pavilion. The main building in the Norway town square looks like a real fourteenth-century fortress in Oslo, Norway.

Norway pavilion at Epcot

There are Kidcot Fun Stops at every pavilion where kids can decorate a bear-shaped park "passport." A cast member can stamp it with a different colorful stamp at each country you visit. So even though you haven't really left the United States, Epcot tries to make you feel like a world traveler.

CHAPTER 6
Animal Kingdom

While the World Showcase celebrates human achievements, Animal Kingdom celebrates the beauty and importance of the natural world.

Five areas help remind us how amazing Earth is and that we must protect it. Discovery Island's Tree of Life is awesome and looks real, but it's not. It stands 145 feet tall and has a trunk that's 50 feet in diameter carved with more than three hundred animals. Artists worked fast to create each animal before the plaster they used dried. The base of the tree had to be super strong to support all of its branches. Yet there had to be room inside for a movie theater to show the film *It's Tough to Be a Bug!* Luckily, an Imagineer came up with the idea of using an oil rig as the tree's skeleton.

Imagineers

The Disney word *Imagineer* is a combination of "imagination" and "engineer." Imagineers combine creativity and technical know-how to turn ideas into rides, attractions, and more. They are okay with failing, because that means they're trying out something new. And if at first they don't succeed, they try, try again. One weekend, an Imagineer was at home puzzling over how to design a new ride called Soarin'. Using his childhood Erector Set, he figured out how to make the ride work!

In Animal Kingdom's Asia land, you'll find the Forbidden Mountain roller coaster at Expedition Everest. At 199 feet, it's Disney World's tallest "mountain." The real Mount Everest is in the Himalayan Mountains, which stretch across India, China, and other countries. Everest is the tallest mountain in the world—29,028 feet! (That's nearly five and a half miles high.) On the Disney World expedition, you can watch for a huge yeti (rhymes with spaghetti). That's a mythical creature that some people believe protects the Himalayas.

There's also a fun outdoor area called The Boneyard at DinoLand U.S.A. where guests can dig up fossils and artifacts. DINOSAUR is a time-travel ride back to sixty-five million years ago when dinosaurs still ruled the planet.

Dino-Sue

In 1990, a paleontologist (fossil scientist) named Sue Hendrickson found a few bones stuck in a cliff in South Dakota. Nearby, she found a few more bones, and still more. They turned out to be the skeleton of a forty-foot-long *Tyrannosaurus rex* with fifty-eight sharp teeth! Most *T. rex* skeletons are missing many bones. This was the most complete one ever found. It's named "Sue" in her honor and is at the Field Museum in Chicago. You'll see a full-size replica of it called Dino-Sue at DinoLand.

At Kilimanjaro Safaris in Africa land, open-air vehicles take you to see animals in their natural habitats. Lions, elephants, zebras, giraffes, and others roam more than one hundred acres, which is about the size of the entire Magic Kingdom.

Park designers do various things to encourage animals to stay in view of guests. For instance, certain rocks in the landscape are heated in winter and cooled in summer so lions will want to hang out there!

The Wildlife Express Train stops at Rafiki's Planet Watch to see how the animals in Animal Kingdom are cared for. Exhibits and cast members are around to explain how people can help animals all over the world. You can ask questions while animals' meals are prepared in a kitchen. Or watch through a glass window as vets examine and treat animals. This is the only Animal Kingdom area where you can pet animals, such as sheep, pigs, and goats.

When animals first come to the Animal Kingdom, they get a checkup in the Disney vet hospital to make sure they are healthy. Vets have an X-ray room, ultrasound equipment, surgery rooms, and labs to do tests. Animals that live here get regular health checkups, somewhat like people do. Gorillas even get their fingernails clipped and their teeth cleaned!

CHAPTER 7
Hollywood Studios

Walt Disney's first love was making movies—short ones, then long ones. And no place is associated with movies more than Hollywood in Los Angeles, California. It is where many of the very first films were made in the early 1900s. So, naturally, movies and TV are the theme of this park.

More than 2,600 brass stars with the names of celebrated entertainers are embedded in the sidewalks of the real Hollywood Boulevard in Los Angeles. Disney World's Hollywood Boulevard is very different but shows various aspects of moviemaking. For instance, the Indiana Jones Epic Stunt Spectacular re-creates live-action scenes from *Raiders of the Lost Ark,* including explosions! Professionals demonstrate stunt fights and whip tricks. Performers tighten their muscles to help avoid injury from stomach punches or kicks. (Even the pretend ones can hurt!)

Walt Disney: One Man's Dream is an exhibit about Walt on Mickey Avenue. You'll see cool historical items like his second-grade school desk and the Audio-Animatronic dancing man. There's a short movie about Walt narrated by actress Julie Andrews, who starred in Disney's film *Mary Poppins*.

Hidden Mickeys

Look up, down, and all around Disney World. In an unexpected place, you might spot a three-circle shape made to resemble Mickey Mouse's head and ears! These shapes are called Hidden Mickeys. They can be almost anywhere—on buildings, rides, even in shadows. Here are a few examples: In the Africa Room of the "it's a small world" ride, some purple ones form a vine near the giraffes; in Epcot's Germany pavilion, look for the Mickey shape in the grass of the miniature village; three-circle designs in the stone near the clock on the exterior of Cinderella Castle casts Mickey's shadow at certain times; and check the asteroids in the Primeval Whirl at Animal Kingdom for Hidden Mickeys, too.

At Echo Lake, Star Tours—The Adventures Continue takes you on a 3-D flight simulation to *Star Wars* locations. At Jedi Training Academy: Trials of the Temple, young guest recruits learn to use the Force while training with lightsabers. When villains appear, these new skills come in handy!

The first *Star Wars* movie didn't open until 1977. So during its early years, Walt Disney World obviously didn't have any *Star Wars* attractions.

But Disney World is always being updated, with some rides, attractions, shops, or restaurants being phased out, while new ones are built.

For instance, Animation Courtyard was once the location where you'd begin a tour to watch Disney animators creating real movies in real studios. The animation studios have been relocated outside of Disney World, and other attractions, such as Voyage of the Little Mermaid, have now replaced them.

CHAPTER 8
Changes and Updates

Many rides or attractions from Disney World's opening day are still around, although they might have a new look. They include Country Bear Jamboree, Dumbo the Flying Elephant, Frontierland Shootin' Arcade, Jungle Cruise, Mad Tea Party, Peter Pan's Flight, Prince Charming Regal Carrousel, Swiss Family Treehouse, The Hall of Presidents, The Haunted Mansion, Tomorrowland Speedway, the Walt Disney World Railroad, the Enchanted Tiki Room, and "it's a small world."

Other opening-day rides have been phased out. One of those is Mr. Toad's Wild Ride. It was a wacky ride in a two-person, open-air buggy that would do things like skid past falling stacks of books in a library and zoom through a fireplace. Some people loved Mr. Toad so much that they protested the closing of the ride with signs and letters that read: "Save the Toad!" Don't worry. If this sounds like a ride for you, you can still go on it in Disneyland.

Did you know there was once a Disney World ride with submarines that actually submerged partly under water with guests inside? It was called 20,000 Leagues Under the Sea, and lasted from 1971 through 1994. It was based on the Disney movie from the book written by Jules Verne. Guests in the subs sat in rows facing outward. Through portholes they saw wonders such as the lost city of Atlantis, magical mermaids, Animatronic sea monsters, coral, lost shipwrecks, and sharks. The submarines required a lot of upkeep, which was part of the reason this ride closed.

Pirates of the Caribbean, a boat ride through a Spanish-style fortress, came to Disney World a couple of years after opening day. Walt Disney helped design this ride, which had been popular at Disneyland since 1967. It has Animatronic singing pirates, and has been updated to include Captain Jack Sparrow from the movies.

One of the newest additions at Disney World is Pandora—The World of Avatar, which opened in Animal Kingdom in 2017. It takes place in a magical world named Pandora, which is protected by tall blue human-like creatures called the Na'vi. One of the rides feels almost like you're flying on a dragon-like banshee!

More big changes are coming to Disney World. Two new lands! An eleven-acre Toy Story Land is scheduled to open in summer 2018 in Hollywood Studios. It will look like a backyard full of giant toys—Andy's backyard. And he has built some fun stuff for you. Like a roller coaster called the Slinky Dog Dash and an Alien Swirling  Saucers attraction with toy flying saucers.

An epic, all-new fourteen-acre land called Star Wars: Galaxy's Edge is also coming to Hollywood Studios in 2019. It'll be like a full-size *Star Wars* movie set of a trading port on a remote planet. It's an "immersive" attraction, which means you're meant to feel like you're really in the *Star Wars* world, meeting smugglers, droids, and characters from the films. Two main attractions are planned, but don't have names yet. In the first one, it's Resistance Troopers vs. Stormtroopers, battling it out. The number-one thing many *Star Wars* fans wish they could do is pilot the *Millennium Falcon*, the fastest ship in the galaxy. In the second ride, it looks like they'll get their wish!

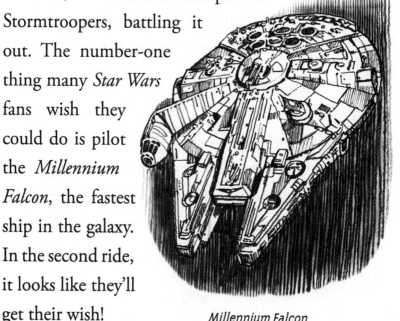

Millennium Falcon

Walt Disney once said, "Disneyland will never be completed. It will continue to grow as long as there is imagination left in the world." The same is true of Disney World. It's always changing and being updated in big or small ways with something old or new—and magical—to enjoy!

CHAPTER 9
Water Parks, Parades, Fireworks, and More

Not only does Walt Disney World Resort keep changing, it has also grown since opening day. It now includes two water parks. Blizzard Beach looks like it used to be a ski resort, until it melted into a wet and wild water land. It even has a chairlift.

Its Summit
Plummet on
Mount Gushmore
is one of the fastest
and tallest waterslides
anywhere in the world,
with a near vertical drop!
Typhoon Lagoon has
whooshing rapids, a sandy
beach, a surf pool, and a
river-raft ride. The speedy
Humunga Kowabunga
slide may cause your hair
to whoosh straight up as you go down it!

Walt Disney never forgot his excitement at
seeing a circus parade go down the main street
of Marceline, Missouri, when he was a boy. He
made parades a part of Disney World, hoping
other kids would be excited, too.

Each afternoon, there's a Disney Festival of Fantasy Parade in Magic Kingdom. Floats wind down the streets starring characters from favorite Disney stories, such as Rapunzel, Cinderella, Belle, Elsa, Anna, Peter Pan, and Wendy, plus performers on stilts and swings. And Mickey and Minnie ride in a big hot-air balloon!

More than one fireworks show lights up Disney World's night skies. IllumiNations—Reflections of Earth is a fireworks show in Epcot. Flames whoosh from a lagoon's Inferno Barge, propelled by propane. A globe appears, its surface lit with images that tell the history of our Earth. Happily Ever After is a state-of-the-art fireworks show at Magic Kingdom's Cinderella Castle. It's got amazing pyrotechnics, lasers, hand-drawn animation, and music that emphasizes the importance of chasing your dreams and finding your happily ever after. Fantasmic! features Mickey and friends at Hollywood Studios.

Cleanup Time!

Disney World's four parks usually close between nine and eleven at night, and the cast members go home. Did you think the parks would get quiet then? Nope. After closing, crews called the "third shift" or "overnight shift" get to work. Gardeners trim trees and hedges and water the hanging pots of flowers. Dim lightbulbs get replaced, shop shelves get dusted. Custodians clean everything! Restrooms get disinfected and scrubbed until they sparkle. Floors are all swept, mopped, vacuumed, and/or polished. Fingerprints get wiped from windows, park benches get washed, seats in the rides get cleaned. Crew members start unrolling long fire hoses to pressure wash every walkway. There might be construction going on to replace broken floor tile or to build a new counter in a shop. Trucks make deliveries of merchandise to shops.

There might even be a camera crew around. Since guests are gone, night is the perfect time to film any indoor commercials. Mechanics do important safety and operational inspections and maintenance. Rides, attractions, and Animatronic characters all get a checkup—almost like going to a doctor. A fun part of this job is getting to test-ride attractions like Space Mountain without crowds around!

Of course, besides providing a lot of fun for guests, the Disney company wants to earn money from the theme parks. In addition to rides and attractions, there are many shops selling Disney souvenirs, as well as fancy or simple restaurants and snack stops throughout Disney World, too. Nearby there's also another huge area of shopping, dining, and entertainment called Disney Springs.

It's designed as four neighborhoods and will soon expand to include more than 150 establishments.

Disney World also has golf courses, campgrounds, a sports complex with a stadium, conference centers, and more. The idea is to offer lots to do, so there'll be more reasons guests will come and stay awhile!

Some of the Special Seasonal Events

At Disney World in the fall, kids can wear a costume and go trick-or-treating at Mickey's Not-So-Scary Halloween Party. In winter, during Walt Disney World Marathon Weekend, runners get to race through all four parks. One year, a couple in the race stopped at Cinderella Castle to get married! In spring, the Epcot International Flower & Garden Festival features a butterfly exhibit, gardens, and outdoor kitchens. And keep your ears open for feathered visitors, who fly to Disney World every year to raise families. They're songbirds called purple martins. They come from three thousand miles away in Brazil.

CHAPTER 10
After-the-Park Fun

In 1971, when Magic Kingdom opened at Disney World, two hotels opened along with it: Disney's Polynesian Resort and Disney's Contemporary Resort. Today there are more than twenty-five hotels at the Walt Disney World Resort, where the fun doesn't have to stop when the park closes.

Many of the hotels are built around a special theme. The outside of the four main buildings at Disney's Art of Animation Resort are covered with colorful murals of characters from *The Lion King*, *The Little Mermaid*, *Finding Nemo*, and *Cars*. The themes are continued inside, with ideas like giant shell-shaped headboards for beds in the

Little Mermaid rooms. There are animation sketches on display in this hotel's lobby. There are drawing classes to learn how to draw Disney characters, too!

Some Disney World hotels are extra fancy, and a little or a lot more expensive than others. Disney's Polynesian Resort along the Seven Seas Lagoon is set up like a South Seas island with palm trees, a sandy beach, and tiki torches.

At night, the Magic Kingdom fireworks light up the sky across the lagoon. The brightly lit Electrical Water Pageant with King Neptune, a sea serpent, and other mythical and real sea creatures parade across the lagoon at night as well!

The Animal Kingdom Lodge is one of the lower-priced hotels. It has an African theme with a huge mud fireplace and hand-carved furniture. Best of all, its lobby and some of the hotel rooms overlook the Kingdom's wildlife preserve, so guests can spot animals or birds.

Families can also camp out at Disney's Fort Wilderness in an RV, tent, or cabin. It's not fancy, but offers fun outdoor things to do such as basketball, canoeing, biking, tennis, and horseback riding.

There's a bigger-than-life bronze statue of Walt holding hands with Mickey Mouse near the center of Disney World. It's called *Partners*. On the statue's base, there's a quote from Walt that reads, "We believe in our idea: a family park where parents and children could have fun—together."

Walt would probably be amazed at how great Disney World worked out. And it was his dream that started it all!

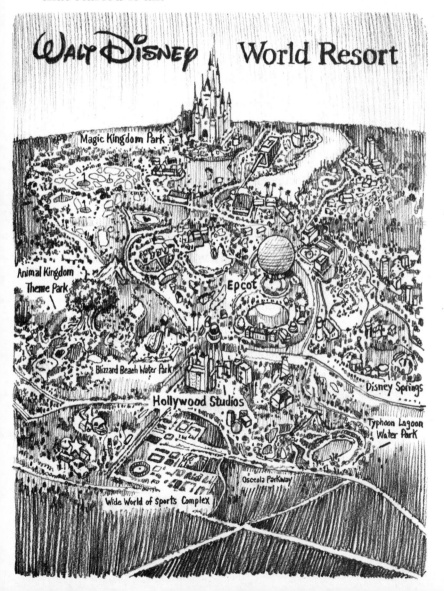

Timeline of Walt Disney World

1901 — Walter Elias Disney is born December 5

1923 — Walt and his brother Roy start the Disney Brothers Cartoon Studio

1928 — Mickey Mouse first appears in a cartoon

1955 — Disneyland opens in California on July 17

— *The Mickey Mouse Club* TV show debuts

1964 — Four Disney exhibits appear at the New York World's Fair

1965 — Walt announces he'll build a new theme park in Florida

1966 — Walt Disney dies December 15 at age sixty-five

1971 — Walt Disney World opens on October 1

1975 — Space Mountain, the first Walt Disney World roller coaster, opens

1982 — Epcot opens October 1

1989 — Disney-MGM Studios (later renamed Hollywood Studios) and Typhoon Lagoon open

1995 — Blizzard Beach Water Park opens

1998 — Disney's Animal Kingdom opens on April 22

2011 — Star Tours—The Adventures Continue opens at Hollywood Studios

2016 — Disney Springs opens

2017 — Pandora—The World of Avatar opens in May

Timeline of the World

1905	First movie theater opens in Pittsburgh, Pennsylvania
1919	Babe Ruth signs on with the New York Yankees baseball team
1940	Bugs Bunny cartoon debuts
1945	World War II ends
1950	Charles Schulz's *Peanuts* comic strip is first published
1958	NASA is formed
1963	Martin Luther King Jr. gives his "I Have a Dream" speech
1967	The first Super Bowl football game is played
1969	Neil Armstrong walks on the moon
	Woodstock, the biggest outdoor music festival of the hippie era, is held in New York
1970	The Environmental Protection Agency is created in the United States
1981	MTV launches as the first twenty-four-hour music-video cable network
2001	Terrorists destroy the World Trade Center in New York City
2008	Barack Obama is elected the first African American US president
2014	Malala Yousafzai is the youngest person ever to win a Nobel Peace Prize
2016	Two stolen paintings by Vincent van Gogh worth $100 million are found

Bibliography

---

*Books for young readers

Apgar, Garry, ed. *Mickey Mouse Reader.* Jackson, MS:
The University Press of Mississippi, 2014.

*Disney Enterprises. *Birnbaum's 2017 Walt Disney World for Kids.*
Glendale, CA: Disney Editions, 2016.

*Foster, Tim. *Walt Disney World Resort Guide to the Magic
for Kids.* Chester Springs, PA: Celebrations Press, 2016.

Gabler, Neal. *Walt Disney: The Triumph of the American
Imagination.* New York: Knopf, 2006.

Korkis, Jim. *Secret Stories of Walt Disney World: Things
You Never Knew You Never Knew.* Orlando, FL: Theme Park
Press, 2015.

Lipp, Doug. *Disney U: How Disney University Develops
the World's Most Engaged, Loyal, and Customer-Centric
Employees.* New York: McGraw-Hill Education, 2013.

Neary, Kevin, and Susan Neary. *The Hidden Mickeys of
Walt Disney World.* Glendale, CA: Disney Editions, 2016.

Sehlinger, Bob, and Liliane J. Opsomer, with Len Testa.
The Unofficial Guide to Walt Disney World with Kids.
Birmingham, AL: AdventureKEEN, 2017.

*Stewart, Whitney. *Who Was Walt Disney?* New York:
Penguin Workshop, 2009.